My Life, I Lapped It Up

My Life, I Lapped It Up

Selected Poems of Edoardo Sanguineti

translated by Will Schutt

Oberlin College Press
Oberlin, Ohio

The FIELD Translation Series, vol. 33
Oberlin College Press, 50 N. Professor Street, Oberlin, OH 44074
www.oberlin.edu/ocpress

Cover and book design: Steve Farkas.
Cover photograph of Edoardo Sanguineti by Giuliana Traverso.

The poems in *My Life, I Lapped It Up* are selected and translated from:

Segnalibro: 1951-1981
Il Gatto Lupesco: 1981-2001
Mikrokosmos: Poesie 1951-2004
Varie ed eventuali: 1995-2010

all by Edoardo Sanguineti and published by Feltrinelli, Milan.

Library of Congress Cataloging-in-Publication Data

Names: Sanguineti, Edoardo, author.
Title: My life, I lapped it up / selected poems of Edoardo Sanguineti ;
   translated by Will Schutt.
Description: Oberlin, Ohio : Oberlin College Press, 2018. | Series: The FIELD
   translation series ; vol. 33 | Includes bibliographical references.
Identifiers: LCCN 2018030335| ISBN 9780997335545 (pbk. : alk. paper) | ISBN
   0997335548 (pbk.)
Subjects: LCSH: Sanguineti, Edoardo—Translations into English.
Classification: LCC PQ4879.A63 A2 2018 | DDC 851/.914—dc23
LC record available at https://lccn.loc.gov/2018030335

Contents

Introduction

In "Poetry and Truth," an essay written in 1995, Edoardo Sanguineti recalls a dinner party thirty years prior at the house of Witold Gombrowicz, when Sanguineti was in his 30s. The exiled Polish novelist, a 60-year-old asthmatic with a heart condition, wouldn't live to see the decade's end. Sanguineti describes immediately recognizing in the "tired and inconsolably ironic" figure in front of him a man who never aspired to the qualities of an acclaimed artist. On the contrary, Gombrowicz was a consummate amateur who, writes Sanguineti, resisted "the religion of the word, sublime 'poetese,' and any form of aristocratic cult surrounding the bard and prophet, celebrated by orphisms and Mallarmé-isms, symbolism and aestheticism" (*Poesia e verità* 169).

Sanguineti's description of the author of *Cosmos* in many ways corresponds to the Genoese poet himself, who would eventually title his final selected poems *Mikrokosmos*. Like Gombrowicz, Sanguineti was suspicious—when not contemptuous—of writers who poeticized or mystified the difficulty of human experience. He began writing, by his own admission, in reaction to an inauthenticity that in his view pervaded the Hermetic and neorealist art practiced in Europe between the wars. By the late 1960s, when *My Life, I Lapped It Up* opens, Sanguineti fully inhabited the role of the wise fool whose playful and elastic language catches out the "crude reality of things," whose clown's mask serves to unmask inauthenticity. "If self-expression has a meaning," he continues in "Poetry and Truth," "it is because it can, it must attempt to express not the inexpressibility of beauty, but the unexpressed truth.... And the truth lies in the anarchistic impulse to lift the veils society places over hardship" (*Poesia e verità* 170).

The anarchistic impulse was instilled in Sanguineti at a young age. Born in Genoa in 1930, he was the only son of Giovanni and Giuseppina Cocchi. When he was four years old, the family moved to Turin after the fascist party forced Giovanni out of a lucrative management position at a bank. Giovanni found a more modest job in Turin working for a typographer. According to Sanguineti, his father never fully recovered from this reversal of fortune.

In Turin Sanguineti grew close to his uncle Luigi Cocchi, a musician and musicologist who had collaborated on the revolutionary weekly *Ordine Nuovo* and was personally acquainted with the Marxist theorist Antonio Gramsci. Gramsci's theory of cultural hegemony—the idea that capitalist society maintains the status quo not by force but by creating a set of ideological values—would later inform

Sanguineti's avant-garde poetics; for Sanguineti, the purpose of reinventing the literary language was to reimagine the culture. As the critic John Picchione writes in *The New Avant-garde in Italy*, Sanguineti was "guided by the conviction that tinkering with the signifiers can eventually effect changes in the signifieds" (127). That tinkering at the lexical level is captured in an early poem from *T.A.T. (Thematic Apperception Test)*:

I write "like so"; (like so):
                    I write: LIKE (on top, first); then: SO (below, after);
(like so: LIKE
                SO); then I write (but the *b* is marred): "boules de lampe torche" (but
the *s* is streaked by the drip of a little drop of color…

Sanguineti found a model of the poet as ideological critic in Dante Alighieri. His doctoral thesis examined the narratives of Malebolge, the eighth circle of hell reserved for grafters, flatterers, and other frauds lite, in the *Divine Comedy*. And in several critical studies written over his lifetime—*Three Dante Studies* (1961), *Dante's Realism* (1966), and *Reactionary Dante* (1992)—Sanguineti sought to rescue the Florentine poet from the then-popular cult of aestheticism, recasting him as an opponent of the political and economic revolutions taking place in fourteenth-century Italy, specifically, the rise of the middle class. Sanguineti, who had begun writing poetry at the height of the nuclear age and the Italian economic boom of the 1950s, believed he was, to paraphrase the critic David Lummus, staring back at Dante from the far end of a narrative woven by capitalist ideology (41).

The Genoese poet found a political alternative to capitalism in Marxism, and unlike other members of the new avant-garde in Italy, he never abandoned Marxist doctrine. Later in life, he held political office. From 1976–81 he served as a city councilor in Genoa, from 1979–83 he was an independent member of Italian Parliament on the Communist Party ticket, and in 2007 he made an unsuccessful bid to become mayor of Genoa. His provocative political stances landed him in trouble from time to time, as when (as reported by *Corriere della Sera*) he compared the victims of the Tiananmen Square massacre to kids "seduced by western mythologies…. All they wanted," he said, "was Coca-Cola."

Sanguineti's political convictions are important for understanding his poetry, yet they were preceded by his interest in art—in all its forms. He initially wanted to become a dancer. That dream was dashed when, as a young boy, he was diagnosed with a fatal heart condition. The diagnosis spelled a housebound childhood. He became so physically frail as a result that, by the time a medical expert revealed that the diagnosis had been made in error, Sanguineti felt the vocation had already slipped his grasp.

The misdiagnosis was, in at least one sense, fortuitous: at the suggestion of his doctors, the family began spending summers in Bordighera, a seaside town close to the French coast. There, Sanguineti fell in with another influential relative, his cousin Angelo Cervetto, who introduced him to jazz. Sanguineti loved music; in addition to novels, plays, critical essays, and several collections of poetry written over a career spanning 50-plus years, he authored several libretti for the experimental composer Luciano Berio. The two collaborated frequently on dizzying mash-ups of literary and musical allusions, like *A-Ronne* and *Coro*. The poem "Little Threnos," with which this book closes, is dedicated to Berio's memory.

Sanguineti often drew inspiration from non-literary artists. "My private appeal to other artistic situations," he wrote in 1961, "was a way of breaking, in solitude, poetic solitude itself" (*Poesia informale?* 202). One visual artist of interest to him was the self-taught painter Carol Rama, whose lusty watercolors and offbeat object art, which incorporated syringes and rubber strips, are reminiscent of the puckish spirit of Sanguineti's later poetry. Another was Enrico Baj, the anarchist and co-founder of the Italian Nuclear Movement, whose kitschy, humorous collages are undergirded by a sense of social justice.

Sanguineti first met Baj in the 1950s, while Sanguineti, then in his early twenties, was writing his first book, *Laborintus*, a 26-part sequence detailing a journey through hell. *Laborintus'* disruptive syntax and assemblage of fragments, foreign languages, and scientific rhetoric marked an important break with the literary models of the day. Its publication in 1956 cleared a path for the experimental Italian poetry of the 1960s and established Sanguineti as a leading intellectual figure of the new avant-garde.

He gained further recognition when he appeared in the controversial 1961 anthology *I Novissimi: Poesie per gli anni '60*, alongside four other young experimental poets. The name *novissimi* reflects the group's tongue-in-cheek personality; literally meaning "the very latest," *novissimi* also refers to the last things: death, judgment, hell, and paradise. For all their avant-garde methods, the group was well aware that the avant-garde itself had historical precedents, that foundations had been broken by early twentieth-century artists, and in Italy, with troubling political results. Nevertheless, it was with great seriousness that the novissimi, Sanguineti in particular, saw their aesthetic transgressions as inextricable from their desire for sociopolitical change. In a collection of essays, *Ideology and Language*, Sanguineti argued that avant-garde literature is, at its core, a "form of protest that… immediately calls into question the overarching structure of social relationships" (*Avanguardia* 62-63). If a break from conventional language led, as he believed, to a change in ideological structures, then it followed that social reality could be transformed too.

It should come as no surprise that Sanguineti admired the lid-blowing modernists of the early twentieth century. His early work, while highly original, owes a debt to Ezra Pound's *The Cantos*. He admired the Futurists and Crepuscolari poets. He also translated Joyce and sampled the opening line of T. S. Eliot's "East Coker" for Berio's vocal ensemble *A-Ronne*. "In my beginning is my end" is a line he would also, on occasion, parody in poems. In 1979's *Scratchpad*, he writes, "I began my beginning many times," part allusion to Eliot, part comment on his own resistance to poetic closure. Almost invariably belonging to longer sequences, Sanguineti's poems end with colons, suggesting that something is to follow, that another beginning is on its way. As he remarked in an interview in the newspaper *L'Unità* in 2002, the poems have "an unfinished flavor." Indeed, reading along, you get the feeling that he is in the grip of one long monologue. Such a reading is made more plausible by Sanguineti's penchant for grouping individual books into omnibus editions. Several appeared in his lifetime, most significantly *Triperuno (Three for One)*, *Il Gatto Lupesco (The Wolfish Cat)*, and *Mikrokosmos*. These three collections of collections roughly divide his career—as he himself saw it—into three distinct phases: tragic, elegiac, and comic.

My Life, I Lapped It Up focuses on the latter two phases. It begins shortly before the 1970s and ends with a poem from his last book, *Any Other Business*, published posthumously in 2010. Collections from these two phases contain, for me, Sanguineti's most psychologically probing and approachable work, when he outgrew the demanding and hyper-allusive manner of *Laborintus* and adopted a messy, diaristic, inclusive mode.

By the early 1970s, Sanguineti had returned for good to the city of his birth, where he taught literature at the University of Genoa and raised four children with his wife Luciana (the couple was married in 1954). His distinctive looks—gaunt, Pulcinella-like—and outspokenness made him an icon of the iconoclastic port city. During this period, he also traveled extensively to participate in literary conferences, experiences he captured in poems that often address Luciana and his children by name. The titles of collections from these years underscore the restlessness and informal candor of the middle poems—*Reisebilder* (1971), *Postkarten* (1977), *Scratchpad* (1979). The middle poems in particular echo the promise made in "Poetry and Truth" to present readers with unadorned reality, opening up the Italian lyric to the unpoetic, the immodest, a style of "no style." Sanguineti describes them in one poem as "minor true episode[s]… fresh-baked, when possible," and the poems amount to a warts-and-all transcription of a life.

That life, and the hardship placed on it by society that the poet sought to unveil—and spoof—may best be described as the mundane, middle-class existence that a socially conscious European writer in the latter half of the last century felt confined to. "The banal, usually, is the hard part," Sanguineti writes in one sendup of fatherly advice ("shower with hot water, shampoo with antidandruff shampoo, watch your penmanship…"). The banal—like ennui in Baudelaire—was a hallmark of his mid- and late-career work, when Sanguineti made art out of mediocre and fleeting encounters, satirical poems out of the not-so-great (though no less painful or ecstatic) lives that society provided.

In his later poems, beginning around 1981's *Casket*, Sanguineti continues to give account of his travels and muse on high and low culture, from the pop star Patty Pravo to the Riace bronzes. The poems are still gathered in numbered sequences (a practice I've abandoned to avoid confusion, since no sequence appears here in its entirety, with the exception of *Mauritshuis*). The titles of some of these collections—*Codicil* (1984), *Rebus* (1987), *Corollary* (1996)—suggest these later poems' even greater use of soundplay and procedural-like method. Some of the sequences are shorter (*Codicil* and *Rebus* each consist of 27 poems compared to *Postkarten*'s 67), and unlike *Reisebilder* and *Postkarten*, whose parts work best in the context of the whole, the later sequences more frequently (though not always) function as collections of stand-alone poems. If there are far fewer of them here, that is partly due to my own shortcomings as a translator; Sanguineti wrote a great deal of difficult poetry. More importantly, I have selected later poems that throw into relief Sanguineti's shift toward the comic, poems in which love is conveyed by a catalog of children's games and cultural history drawn by a string of rhyming, alliterative and near-anagrammatic words:

in my life I've already seen blazers, beetles, an inferno upended by Doré,
cholera, colors, seas and marble stones: and a square in Oslo, the Grand Hôtel
des Palmes, bourses, busts:
     I've already seen blackjack, anagrams, hecto-
grams, fruitcakes, racetracks, jackpots, monuments to Mazzini, chicks and children,
Ridolini:
     I've already seen the firing squads of the Third of May (reproductions only,

in black and white), the tortured in June, the massacred in September, the hanged in March,
in December: and my mother's sex and my father's: the void, veritas, unarmed
worms, and thermal spas…

The poems, mid and late, are anything but banal. They possess lines of manic energy:

(oh, get on with it, pop your pills):

waggishness:

2 or 3 inches of fate will do me (and then some):

and impromptu panache:

…Octavio isn't the man he once was
(nor am I, naturally, nor is anyone): like Marie Jo, for example, who lost
her famous black hat in London, in a museum…:

These qualities upend the cut-and-dried character of straight realism. Many of the poems share the
sensibility of Dutch genre painting: they are spirited depictions of daily scenes stripped of pretenses.
(Hence my inclusion of a group of poems based on paintings in the Mauritshuis.)

The poems aren't just fun and games; their humor is sympathetic to the human comedy and en-
gaged in earnest self-inquiry. The constant parenthetical interruptions and colons without enumera-
tion reflect, in some cases, the conflicted desires of a speaker who wants both to slip free of the self
and arrest the self:

what (I wonder) do I seek in myself so that I run from myself, thus running, forever
at a gallop? it's me, I know:

Not included here, beside his first three collections, are Sanguineti's experiments in traditional forms:
the ballads, abecedarians, acrostics, "semi" sonnets, and "double" or "triple" haiku that he composed,

by and large, from 1982 till his death in 2010. Their exclusion, too, accounts for the shortage of later work in this selection. They are interesting and demanding poems, but my more humble ambition has been to provide English-language readers with a sense of continuity, even if that continuity comes at the expense of range. I also hope that this book will inspire future translators to take up Sanguineti and the new avant-garde Italian writers who remain little known to American readers otherwise familiar with the generation of Italian poets that came before them, like Eugenio Montale or Giuseppe Ungaretti.

In translating Sanguineti's poems, I have tried to be as faithful as possible to the original work yet am also aware of the importance of keeping an ear out for ways to enrich the English and convey a sense of Sanguineti's stylistic ingenuity. One major challenge of translating this poet is to convey his disruptive, anarchic sensibility without sounding so stiff as to read like a translation, lest the reader attribute purposeful awkwardness in the original to awkwardness sometimes found in translation. This too helps explain my decision to begin this selection later in Sanguineti's career, when the language recovers a semblance of linearity and straightforwardness.

A related demand is capturing Sanguineti's poetic impropriety. None of the collars are starched, few of the edges sanded. The poems are often garrulous and devoid of "good" manners. Just as some readers might consider their subjects in bad taste—lurid, goofy, seemingly inconsequential—some writers might question the taste of their poetic methods: hyper-alliteration, redundancy, harsh enjambment. That impropriety can take the form of repetitive throwaway phrases like "and that," "so then," "here now," or funny coinages like "muscolame," a cross between the Italian words for "muscles" and "assortment" ("muscle-mush," in my translation). Many poems appear purely driven by soundplay (italics mine):

> ...e sto
>
> affun*ato*, carrucol*ato* (con gli occhi *tutti* a pos*to*, *to*lti i denti, se sono un B,
> *tutta*via):
> > (ma in fondo sarò un *A*, per cari*tà*, va' *là*, gonfio di quali*tà*):

> ...and I'm
>
> cabled together, pulleyed up (my eyes all set, my teeth taken out, if I'm a B,
> so be it):
> > (at heart I'm an A, please, you don't say, puffed up with good stuff):

Where the volume is turned up, I've occasionally allowed myself detonative wiggle room to amplify the sense of sound. An extreme but rare example of this is in the poem "What (I wonder)." Sanguineti writes "scappo…(dal mio essere morto): (un *molle* morto): (scappo da una mia *mala* morte)." How should a translator simultaneously convey the opposite meaning and phonetic proximity of the words "molle" (feeble, soft) and "mala" (evil, bad)? A literal translation is too ponderous for a poem about galloping away from the endgame: "I run… (from my death): (a feeble death): (I run from an evil death)." My translation reads: "I run… (from my death): (a sweet death): (a sleep-with-the-fishes death)." While betraying the letter, I hope that Sanguineti would appreciate the combination of poetic and popular diction, and I justify the betrayal by telling myself that, in addition to the echo of "sweet" and "sleep," my translation also retains the original poem's out-of-breath quality.

"The dream… is to say it all," Sanguineti writes elsewhere, as if to explain his poems' volubility. Yet despite their chaotic, grab-bag quality, the poems are also carefully choreographed. Take, for example, the following poem, which has a lyric shapeliness even as it suggests that disorder—cut-up, dunked and gulped—is the order of the day:

> into this shoddy retiro filled with fairground booths (a dancer in yellow and green
> and white was defying the mud, limply pirouetting), we fell, first three of us, then
> four: (the discovery of paper models—to cut up with desperate, entirely
> Iberian tenacity—and soft donuts—to dunk and gulp—occurred shortly after,
> with the wordless, lakeside quack-quacks, which are, on the other hand,
> universal):
> > but it's late, it's dark out, they're closing down, and the taxi's on its way:

The poem's sense of alienation is immediately signaled by the foreign word "retiro," Spanish for retreat or refuge. And by the end of the poem we hear an echo of that foreign tongue in the "quack-quacks" of ducks by the lake. Like those ducks, reduced to noises, the poem itself *says* nothing, refusing to extract insight from or transfigure experience. Instead the experience remains a non-event; we drift here and there before cutting away.

As for the dancer, his bright attire calls to mind Sanguineti's go-to pathetic hero, the acrobat or clown, a symbol of the artist as partially valiant and partially preposterous. His attempt to execute a graceful pirouette, though defiant, seems woefully out of place.

xvi

In a short questionnaire included as an appendix to *Mikrokosmos*, Sanguineti confessed that his favorite food was raw herring, his favorite childhood toy the rocking horse, his favorite poets Lucretius, Dante, and Baudelaire. What he held most dear was his wife Luciana. His greatest defect was obstinacy. His motto, "ideology and language." When asked what he would like to be, he responded that in the past he had wanted to be a dancer. When asked how he'd like to die, he responded, "lucid" (*Risposte* 326-38). The enfant terrible of postwar Italian poetry lived to be 79.

Will Schutt

Works Cited

Frenda, Angela. "*Tienanmen, tra Sanguineti e la sinistra scoppia la crisi.*" *Corriere della Sera*, 23 Jan. 2007.

Lummus, David. "Edoardo Sanguineti's New Dante." *Edoardo Sanguineti: Literature, Ideology and the Avant-Garde*. Eds. Paolo Chirumbo and John Picchione. London: Routledge, 2013.

Palieri, Maria Serena. "*Sanguineti: io do il cattivo esempio.*" *L'Unità*, 22 Nov. 2002.

Picchione, John. *The New Avant-garde in Italy: Theoretical Debate and Poetic Practices.* Toronto: University of Toronto Press, 2004.

Sanguineti, Edoardo. "*Avanguardia, società, impegno.*" *Ideologia e linguaggio*. Milan: Feltrinelli, 2001.

—-. "*Poesia e verità.*" *Ideologia e linguaggio*. Milan: Feltrinelli, 2001.

—-. "*Poesia informale?*" *I Novissimi: Poesie per gli Anni '60*. Turin: Einaudi, 1961.

—-. "*Risposte a un questionario.*" *Mikrokosmos*. Milan: Feltrinelli, 2004.

from *T.A.T. (Thematic Apperception Test)*

"I write 'like so'"

I write "like so"; (like so):

                          I write: LIKE (on top, first); then: SO (below, after);

(like so: LIKE

                 SO); then I write (but the *b* is marred): "boules de lampe torche" (but

the *s* is streaked by the drip of a little drop of color, which spills down,

over a little floating drop:

                       down, from a pig's mouth): and many circles

start to spread; downward, concentrically; as in a blue pool (if the little stones

spill over us, in us, down us); (the little drops):

                            (like so):

from *Reisebilder*

"at 6:15 p.m. Vasko phones"

at 6:15 p.m. Vasko phones: you awake? he asks: sure, I say: and
I've already talked to my wife: (so the telegram was a total waste):
(but clearly that's no matter):
                                and I've already written the second poem of the day
(today, June 3rd):
                great, says Vasko, you've really been blessed
this week, then: (this week: of Knaak-Poetry):

"where are the forty poets"

where are the forty poets, asked Tadeusz (or maybe it was
Yehuda speaking): the forty who never meet up: (and will save poetry):
and where are the four poets struck dead by a blazing sword
of whiskey: the four shut inside B. M. Scheffers' (or some other neighborhood
restaurant) for a little bridge of words?
                         and what kind of renga was that
if it was born without your eyes, without your gums? (not even an ordinary
Dolle Mina was around to place in the middle: to copy down: as I said,
with words):
             but now I copy your body as I saw it in a dream
tonight: I copy it with these words:
                     avec ces petites proses en poème:

"that one who sleeps"

that one who sleeps in a corner of the living room, so full of life: that one who adores
the polished parquet: we all feel it keenly: in four months
she'll become an enormous thing:
                          we'll return her to the shopkeeper in slacks from the Café
Belvedere, in the courtyard at the spa, this impossible tortoise inside a massive
cardboard box (with several air holes) for Pelikan felt-tip pens, with a wedge
of lettuce (plus a slice of tomato):
                          this monster that does not speak:

"I'm more Slavic than Tadeusz"

I'm more Slavic than Tadeusz if it's true Italians are Slavs, and if Slavs
are the ones who caress with their words, saying: wie geht es dir? (and other such
greetings: which are, as I say, caresses):

I caressed the Pole Tadeusz Różewicz
one night at Adriaan's house, scribbling down a note for him that read precisely:
wie geht es dir? (and smiling at him from afar: and greeting him with a wave):
(since he hadn't touched a drink in over a year: and in a year composes on average
only two or three poems):

(but I'll read his old verses, it's a pact
we made between us: to determine if the verses are Slavic, Polish or sick):

(today I get the sense that the Germans are rather Spanish: the right people for corridas,
for crying olè!: and cockfights—and for literaturwissenschaft):

(like Archibaldo de la Cruz, I dream up crimes I don't know how to commit:
a fragile platonic erotomaniac, inhibited pornographer: a poet):

"the two corpses displayed in the basement"

the two corpses displayed in the basement (if you run and jump like that,
you're going to fall into a tomb: better take my hand) are categorically
prehistoric: (I'll read you where they found them if you'd like):
                                                              I suppose
if they're here in the right wing of the Museum für Vor- und Frühgeschichte
(the left wing of Charlottenburg Palace), then they're the property of the Bundesrepublik:

but it's highly unlikely, Michele, that one day such interest in us
will survive:
                we'll never be buried between mammoth tusks: no one will place
that stone you see, big as a baby's fist, in the empty space
where my heart was:
                (look for me where I am: in the tattered *Totentanz* in the Marienkirche,
the last figure facing the interior, forever hidden under white plaster):

"I'd never heard so many hallelujahs"

I'd never heard so many hallelujahs as I did in that gaststätte by the green square
off Spandauer Damm:

              one Herr Hauptmann, shitfaced, of the Führer's Luftwaffe,
suspecting we were English, detested us: and after a hundred hallelujahs (and a dozen
Dovers: the man had dived a thousand feet off the white cliffs in his day),
he turned out to be the son of a baritone who sang Handel: (there's still
a marvelous album of his, apparently, ein romantische platte):

                           (and he sent our gnarly,
nasty kotoletts und würstchen down the wrong pipe):

                    in Goethe's *Tag- und Jahreshefte*,
in the year 1789, we read about the narrator/traveler's purpose:
(und da objekt so rein als nur zu tun wäre in mich aufzunehmen):

"the Aeolian harps do not play for you"

the Aeolian harps do not play for you:
                              I heard one (circa 1800)
in room ten of the Museum of Musikinstrumente at the Institute
für Musikforschung: a very brief, very rare clip recorded
on tape:
          the academic team of Asian specialists (one man
and many women), enchanted by every tafelklavier and hammerflügel
(the guide played them a nocturne by an obscure precursor of Chopin),
had already vanished:
                     though not exactly lying in a flowery meadow
you were, at least, sitting on a bench in the garden in Bundesallee
among old women armed with canes who spoke "un petit francais":
you were ermüdet, unruhig, schlafsuchend, anyway, with your excruciating
headache, with your amorousness and nerves all shot:
                           and simply dreamt
of hopping on the S-Bahn and reaching this oasis in Pichelsberg:
(so that Goethe's siegelring, display case 26, exists for me only in a catalog):

"August 1ˢᵗ (a Sunday)"

August 1ˢᵗ (a Sunday), everyone in Spandau for the afternoon, with Bisinger
and his friend from Munich (or around Munich): (a student of architecture,
she makes us explore centuries of bastions and bricks):
                                        on our guided tour
we take in, besides hedgerows of nettles, the ruins of giftgaslaboratorien, which were
operative in the lagers: broken pipes, mouse nests (and half-smashed
plaster casts of the Brandenburg Gate horses):
                                        (from the haven
of a beer hall, where they pour green froth in a glass, there drifts the divine
music of coins cascading from a slot machine):

"during a rather dreary, and, at times, abstractly theoretical"

during a rather dreary, and, at times, abstractly theoretical evening conversation
(I don't recall the particulars now), I felt we were marked
by a mortal moral disease:
                              I had been talking about the degradation
of everyday privacy: (and I should have been more insistent about our having
let ourselves go like this, crushed between the pathetic and vulgar,
locked in the deformed bourgeois experience):
                                        maybe I exaggerate: yet something's
amiss, even in the way we carry ourselves (see how you're sitting, for example,
at this moment): as well as when I tell you about young Goethe
in Leipzig badgering everyone to find out what exactly erfahrung was,
that thing they all said he lacked:
                              (and how an officer on leave answered him):

"the ugly purple corpse I lug behind me"

the ugly purple corpse I lug behind me, with all I've got,
down a blind upholstered hallway: (still inside the big house on Corso Matteotti,
it appears):
                    swaddled in rags and damp towels
(somehow my brothers-in-law have a hand in this absurdly apocryphal deposition
involving copper and tin tubs): (and involving secret agents,
go figure, and similar riffraff watching over me):
                                        (half a foot,
packed up and putrid, fell to the floor as we wound our way through
the dream: a large, rough chunk of soap fat): (and I don't know anymore
where to hide it, or how, if you don't help me): I'm telling you now
that I've suddenly got it: (and you can get me): this is my corpse:

from *Postkarten*

"it all started with a stupid story"

it all started with a stupid story of mistaken coats at a restaurant
called Rosetta's: (and with you running blind, past the offices
of Alitalia, distracted, absentminded):
                                        hey, my dear, you at the Bar d'Amore,
it seems to me there's little to laugh about if it's so easy for us to lose
our identity, our clothes, our distinguishing features, our points
of reference, bearings, common sense:
                                        (we're lost in the world again,
each in his way: and as he deserves): (and if I write to you from the airport
in Capodichino, departing for Amsterdam on flights AZ 424 and AZ 382,
it's superstition pure and simple: for no other reason, really, none at all):

"you haven't changed a bit"

you haven't changed a bit (but Berlin is still Berlin too), my gypsy star
tells me as soon as she sees me:
                                        and goes on to read not my hand
but my hands, plural, my life, rather, all of it, scrupulously:
                                                        the reading's held
at the Paris Bar, by the way, in the presence of an Austrian (who filched the face
of poor B.B. when he was young) (over a bowl of onion soup and a rare steak):
and her husband (who shows real promise, in what field I forget):
                                                        I dispute some dubious
low blows, ignore the question insinuating bigamy, point out a deep-cut
cross (which means I've done things that will live on after me, maybe):
and conclude that 2 or 3 inches of fate will do me (and then some):

"you say that Anna says"

you say that Anna says my eyes shine when she whispers that you
are pregnant:
                    (and that Dr. Tafuri, after April's test came back negative,
sensed my profound unhappiness over the phone):
                                                but I'm a fatalist
is what I say (and, as you know, act impassively): (and go to impossible lengths
to act that way):
                    but it's all because I chase after myself, in reality, laughably, breathless
from the pursuit: in other words, because I don't deserve me: (I don't deserve you, Luciana):

"put it back on its feet, the culture"

put it back on its feet, the culture:
                                    I proposed in the foyer of the Eliseo
Friday: it was a mini-slogan, see, tossed out there, the idea of a bottom-up,
rather than top-down, hierarchy:
                                    (and to remind everyone: if we divided
the electoral body by profession, housewives would come out ahead with 32.8%):

"what a shame"

what a shame, dear children (and what horrors you missed),
that you never saw your grandfather with his cobbler's chest
(called pectus excavatum), as he shook and babbled, as if he had
tombé en enfance, kissing the doctors' hands:
                                                his parting words
weren't spoken by him but by Carol, over the phone,
speaking of her mother now in a coma, when she said she was a woman
possessed of such tact:
                        and added: manners are everything:

"I taught my sons to know my father"

I taught my sons to know my father was an extraordinary man (they can
tell it like that, to someone, over time): and then, that all
men are extraordinary:
      and that of a man there survive, I don't know,
about ten phrases maybe (adding it all up: the tics,
the memorable remarks, the slips of tongue):
         and those are the lucky ones:

"this pillow is a butterfly"

this pillow is a butterfly: that one, I don't know (must be an eye, I guess,
or a fish, like sole: that's it, it must be a fish eye):
                                                    (dear Elena,
my daughter continues to chew up her pillows: so we've put them
out of reach, for now, in the window frames):
                                                    she comes home
laden with things: they spill from her bag: a red on red, handstitched
(silk and wool) Guidotti piece: set designs (photocopied) for *Orlando*,
for *I masnadieri*:
                        it's a true story, by which I mean she gets it all
from her mother (who's dead), who used to make pillows, etc.
(but more abstract, etc.):
                                    even the coat she's wearing, look (and the hair
on her head: like Olympia, maybe, or Alcina):
                                                    and now where'll they wind up,
the drawings, the shawls, and the rest?
                                    in a gallery in Milan: and onto the world's stage:

"let's talk, please, about life's pleasures"

let's talk, please, about life's pleasures for once (I said
on Monday around 11 to van Rossum's wife): (a German from Munich,
under 30, I think, with skin white as egg white):
                                        and the first
pleasure is to screw, sure: and then for me, to sleep in the sun (as I was sleeping
just now, I told her, before she arrived: bare-chested as she sees me, bare-
foot, etc.): and the third's to drink wine (French, if possible, like the wine
we drank on Saturday with Berio, and Friday too, in Rotterdam and here):
(so I concluded maybe paradise is screwing in the sun, drunk on Saint-Emilion):

"the final account on the return flight"

the final account on the return flight is this:

                                                                 I really ran

(my mouth) with everybody: I saw no end of old faces

(including mellow Inneke, imagine that, who when she smiles now

has crow's feet, and the same old witness by her side:

                                                                   she came by

to thank me, in the end, for my early poems: since I'd re-read them

at the Doelen, after the raw herring and fanfare of troubadours, and after

the lights came back on in the room):

                                                       and Octavio isn't the man he once was

(nor am I, naturally, nor is anyone): like Marie Jo, for example, who lost

her famous black hat in London, at a museum…:

"I carry a basket on my head"

I carry a basket on my head, a load with holes: and a cockscomb protrudes from the top
(like the chimney stacks in Vršac, alert to every wind, like the ones I saw
from the windows in the theater, I think, or in the museum, near the vintner's
gizmos):
        the rest is edible animals, bottles of Vignac,
and wines from Banat: (the miniature guzla's in the suitcase with a micro-
peasant made of wood, who's laughing in a lined box): and so I'm hauling in
some symbols for you:
        because the piglets are your inner lips
(the prettiest piece of tail in Europe, as your mother says), the pheasants are your eyes,
the fish your feet and brow:
        but on this spit I hold in my hand
is me, again, skewered twice, ready to be roasted, laid out like a chicken:
(the title block in the almanac promises you life:
        and toasts you, bon appétit):

"to prepare a poem"

to prepare a poem, take "a minor true episode" (when possible,
fresh daily): there's a similar recipe in Stendhal, I know, but in the end
it has a whole different flavor: (and I'd lose at least an hour now,
here, looking for an apt quotation: and, frankly, I don't want to):

                                         it helps to clear up
space and time: an exact date and meticulously drawn place are, in any case,
the most desirable ingredients: (ditto characters, who should be crafted in accord
with their vital stats: and objectively recognizable):

                                  I named Stendhal:
but for style there's no need for civic codes today (and therefore, naturally,
no Napoleon): (think instead of Gramsci in the *Notebooks* or *Letters*, yet
seasoned with a little spice: the kind you might find back there in the kitchen
next to young Marx): and voilà, we have a tasty edible dish, a verifiable specialty:
(verifiable in the sense the word has in Brecht, I think, in certain notes
from his *Arbeitsjournal*): (as for the (fundamental) V-effect, that can be whipped up
by modest means): (like here, with a dash of Artusi and Carnacina):
in conclusion, poetry consists, all told, of this type of work: wedging the words
between quotation marks: laboring to make them memorable, like jokes,
clever and brief: (which are imprinted on the mind with a side of socially adequate
signifiers): (like line breaks, alliteration, and, why not, the usual metaphors):
(which combined come to signify:

                            careful, o reader, and commit me to memory):

"poetry's still practicable, probably"

poetry's still practicable, probably: don't you see I practice it,
in any case, practically like this:
                                    with everyday (and daily news like)
poetry: yet this journaling (and, if you like, journalistic) poetry
is clearer than that article by Fortini that rattles on about the clarity
of newspaper articles, if you saw the *Corriere* on Monday the 11th,
entitled, as a matter of fact, "Why It's Hard to Write Clearly" (and that
even states, for christ's sake, that clarity is like virginity and youth): (and that
we must lose them, apparently, to find them): (but I say at bottom
it's better to lose them than find them):
                                    because now I dream of sinking headfirst
into absolute anonymity (now that I've lost everything, or almost): (and
this means, I think, deep down, that I'm dreaming absolutely of dying
this time, you know):
                    today my style is to have no style:

"one writes especially"

one writes especially so that someone else can write, I said
to one of my children the other day: (because by now we're kind of trying to write
the complete works of humankind, all together, deep down):
                                                        and then
another day I related all of this to another of my children, and that child told me:
that's how it should be:
                         and then yesterday that child told me one lives
especially so, etc.: (we were swept up in the night, in the roar of the sea
off Corso Italia, overlooking the beach, at a place called Domenico's, I think):
(and I said, I think, nothing back):
                                    (and then, look, dear child, put that way, the thing
becomes too trivial, too unbearable, etc.):
                                         (and then, dear children, that same day
I took this other child of mine, mentioned above, first, and slapped him hard, for love):

"my father's voice is recorded"

my father's voice is recorded on a tape labeled "Venice '66":
(the flipside features a Mozart symphony):

                                        on the tape is a series
of phone calls from that time: my three boys, my wife, various relatives
of my wife, and a couple of her friends wound up on that wiretap
(there's even my mother-in-law ordering a bottle of Lurisia from a grocer
in Turin, an Emilian is my guess):

                              the electrifying clip (which electrified me
on Tuesday at the height of my unhappiness): (and was a typical trait of his):
(that would determine many aspects of my life): (I'm quoting from memory now)
is when he says to Federico:

                              when others are happy, I'm happy too:

from *Scratchpad*

"I live like a mouse"

I live like a mouse: (a real mouse): (that nibbles crusts): (with its tough
gums): (and these days digests this 1700s plateau that ranges, I don't know,
from Restif to Rousseau):

        and on the 8th inst the problem of happiness
is floated once more: I return to lecturing you: the precept is: swim naturally
in history: (oxymoronically speaking): (like that day I lost you at the station
in Pisa): (in that pathetic scene): (with you among the young mob,
amid the goodbyes):

        (between pleasure and reality, between
desire and false consciousness): naturally nevertheless: (i.e., befitting human
nature): (i.e., befitting work): (daywork):

        you sounded rattled to me
one Sunday morning on the phone: (excessively rattled): (excessively rattling
to me): (and: I can hang up, I thought): (and instead I told you: come on,
hang in there): (navigating the inconceivable labyrinthe): (from a Duomotel
in Milan no less): (du coeur humain):

        (I spoke to Maria just now): (on the phone): (I evoke,
I invoke): (over a lonely dinner): (and: if you must know, I've always suffered
from loneliness): (and: always will) (and: I nibble and spit):

        (my trap, I feel it, awaits me):
(a basement brand, with a spring-loaded bar for the skull):

        (and, like that, snap, crack):

"I began your Chinese notebook"

I began your Chinese notebook to close out (and kick off) the year
working: (it's a superstition, ultimately, you know me): (and corresponds
to old myths and rituals of mine): and I throw my little Big Party for me:
(but what Benjamin, in this regard, didn't calculate, is the technological "aura"): (there exists
a technical distance, to be exact, that reproduces, in reproductions, the taboo): but
about that, more anon):
                    I've already filled a few pages with annotations, with notes
that remain a mess: (regarding, in part, the opening chapter, and,
in part, the entire structure): (but I don't want to give away too much: you'll see,
it's better, in the end, all at once):
                    I began my beginning many times:
there's a scene where an I (or a he, I'm still not sure which, and it's not that important)
runs away from home: (I think I'll call it, no kidding, the House of the Three Girls):
(the whole thing has an operetta-like mood, that's a fact, in the opening): (even if those three
girls are really two girls plus a gigantic cross-dressing boy: he'll be in
a "habit d'Armenien," like the one, I suppose, Clarice wears in *Les Aventures de* ***
when she runs after Clorante in vol. 1 ("je vais la suivre à mon tour"): (I'm reading it
right now, see): (sometimes I think: as soon as I get going I could write to you
like this from here to eternity): (which is an illusion, naturally): (in fact
I'll stop right there):
                    (but the tentative title, I almost forgot, is *The Crossword*):

"aber, I'm telling you, son"

aber, I'm telling you, son, that we've arrived at the culmination, or almost
(to be here like this, in these finsteren zeiten, as we should be): and that
what we're being forced to tolerate, now, is an overdose of reality: and that
if a poet is going to do any damn thing, by chance, with times this dark
and empty, it will be an unfrocked poet, undercover: (and white collar): (okay,
but one who tells us how things really stand): (and doesn't bother to ask wozu
first): (and no nachsicht after): (who, in other words, can be translated
loosely): (and who'd always half-rejected lustprinzip, like a pure epicurean):
(like an aspiring historical materialist, if you prefer my preferred self-definition
today):
     (I'm writing with both feet planted in a mall while you wheel around,
drenched and drugged, from one bus terminal to another): (I'm telling you:
aber, at least tolerate your life a little):
          (oh, get on with it, pop your pills):

"a slogan slipped"

a slogan slipped out of my mouth the other day in the heart of a debate:
it goes like this: Marxists of Italy, Unite:
                                        (but I have the feeling that, in general,
there are just a few of us left): (and even if we huddled together, we wouldn't form
the great mass you'd think we would): elsewhere I've said and written
that I've always preferred real socialism, for all its faults, to unreal socialism:
with age comes apathy, I'm afraid: and yet, utopia blown,
at least at rapid fire I distance myself from sirens, monsters, and chimeras:

"I'll return to my last poem"

I'll return to my last poem if you call, since I didn't explain myself well: (but I'll keep it
brief, it's late, everyone here is asleep, I'm tired, and I have to be up early
tomorrow: but let's get on with it):
                                        I meant to say (to you) that to me Marxism
is becoming scarce around here, and every day someone's watering it down,
defiling it, twisting it, losing sight of it: (and I get the impression that these are dark times
full of widespread panic): (and what worries me isn't the drop in the polls
but the unraveling of an ideology):
                                        giving up utopia caused me no pain:
today I simply think, with a sobering dose of realism, that basic
survival—having a house, food, clothes, school, work, pension, etc.—here, now,
will be a hopeless venture for citizens: (and there isn't much more
to ask of this world: and maybe this is all the utopia we'll get): and
now I'll add:
                        I believe in the historical compromise, in the Italian road
to socialism, in proletarian dictatorship (in its various and, if you will,
endless historical incarnations, agreed):
                                        and in Antonio Gramsci:
(and that bit about age and apathy, mind you, I deduced from him, on a hunch):

"you kept saying, text and translation"

you kept saying, text and translation, and saying again, from the hospital bed
(after revisiting Leningrad), to the nurse, to the doctor, and to me,
this, which broke my spirit:
                              I'm a humane (I'm misquoting) person:
you're a humane person: so am I (a humane person, always):
                                                            I couldn't
weep (and I can't): I know you have yet to distinguish between a cold soul
and a rugged soul, a hard heart and a heart sealed shut: to you I'm made
of stone: (to you, to many, to too many) I'm brazen-faced: (and suffer and moan):

"today I recognized in myself"

today I recognized in myself (by which I mean, in a passage in Bergson) the precise
traits of a master criminal:
                    I'm referring to the idée angoissante qu'un détail
a été négligé: (I'm saying I live in (and on) the perpetual, minute recuperation of minutiae
that has been lost (and lost sight of) in life): (I live, as I have the habit of confessing
in my Quo Vadis pocketbook, agenda planning): I suspect the ground could open
under my feet when my time is through:
                    I monitor and police myself (and clearly
punish myself), examining my old days and new, looking for the clue that will reveal myself:

"if we die for love, then you and I are dead"

if we die for love, then you and I are dead:

                        we're stages of a serial story (or rather,
a national bestseller deliberately disguised as a harlequin romance): (or rather,
a risqué novel): (a rosé): (or rather, a vigorous couple, two vegetating old folks
pressed in the torpid press of our silver anniversary): (a step or a hair's breadth
away from a noir): (we're practically a roman rouge): and let's be clear, we produce
plenty of pain and pity:

                    I'll communicate the necessary coordinates: I'm returning from Como,
it's the 26th of September, 9:37 p.m., I've asked the waiter for the check, I'll catch the 9:50
express, and I understood you: that's all:

                         because it's impossible for you and me
to tolerate any further the insoluble ambivalence in the wine of life we live:
this life, or rather: (life): (washed up, watered down): and if I tell you and if I write to you
that I'm nothing but a contemporary so that you get me, or get it, if that's okay, then we
possess, all in all, 25% of our natural heirs, as things stand:
so, as I bid you a fond farewell, I'll add:

                      if we live for love, then we're alive:

from *Daybook*

"the sad one, the inconstant one"

the sad one, the inconstant one, the aggressive one, the one who died:
(my Tropic of Cancer: my Ring of Saturn): the demure one,
the oddball, the nutcase:
                        I want them all here, now, together, to eat me:
my slit wrists, my smutty tongue, my docile digits, my ailing liver:
(and my heart, as per usual, in shards): (and my brain
already shriveled, and my sex long limp):
                        all the rest is yours
if a rest remains after so much sucking, and if you linger in the kitchen,
the last one, to clear me away:
                        weary one, nervous one, superstitious one, the tender:

"I shave half your beard today"

I shave half your beard today in the bathroom mirror (and often go
against the grain):
                I'm no virtuoso with shaving cream and a razor, as
you can tell, see, from extensive evidence, the stubborn nicks
on my face: (yet all in all, my son, I get by well enough, I think):
(and now a few last tips: shower with hot water, shampoo with antidandruff
shampoo, watch your penmanship, keep an eye on your waistline and wallet,
tie your tie with care):
               the banal, usually, is the hard part:

"feeling bad did me good"

feeling bad did me good: (I live, for my low blood pressure, under
too much pressure: and in a state of depression):
                                                  between angina and anguish exists
a well-known etymological (and physiological and psychological) nexus: (but now's
not the place to exaggerate my psychosomatic manias):
                                                  when I slip under the covers
and face myself by myself with a thermometer in my body (up my ass,
in my mouth, under my armpit, by my groin, which is always the same ailment),
I'm performing my spiritual exercises, I'm taking my tests of consciousness:

"in the beginning was the calculation"

in the beginning was the calculation:
                              our planned investment in affection
made in a few blocks of sweet irredeemable bonds with twenty-five-year terms
and an average rate of procreation every X number of years (which later on
could be negotiated, and indexed, separately):
                              all the conditions, the official
tenor of the contract's fine print, I remember very vaguely:
as hazy as a hazy dream: (but the result, in any case, is right here
under our farsighted and swollen eyes):
                              you're my sheltering asset
(but for me the cost of living increases every day): I'm not in crisis mode,
my little ingot, not exactly: (and our private capital is safe): to me you're more
golden than gold, as the poets say:
                              (but the devaluation I endured is enormous):

"you have to want to die"

you have to want to die a little if you want to partake of life:
(for so long, in so many forms, and in utter vain I've tried
to plant this sentence in my kid's head): (he scares easily): (it's all
catch and release, I repeat):
                              (and the mirror opposite of any link
between amour de vivre and relative désespoir): (the only thing
I agree with Camus on is his encomium of the chambre d'hôtel
as the best place to work, to carve out a life):
                                       (therein, i.e., herein,
lies my true serait egal de mourir):
                    NOTA BENE:
the philosophies ironiques will be the ones to birth les œuvres
passionnées: but, to be clear, what matters to me is the inverse:

"the dream, which says it all"

the dream, which says it all, is to say it all:
                                        I unfurl my tongue and am unsure
if I should be ashamed, but I will say that I'm making my peace, small step
by small step, with the world:
                                        (that my deep, innate horror of existence has been growing
gradually smaller for some time now): (and that I feel, with critical realism,
and cynicism, partially at ease, in the long run, taking the long view,
with my thighbone, my impulses, with carnations, habeas corpus, and firemen,
with Schelling and with Schiller):
                        my impatience is my genius:

"I readjusted to glasses"

I readjusted to glasses (which I'm now required to wear when I drive)
in just a couple of days: I see everything more clearly: (but truth is,
nothing has improved: a traffic light is still a traffic light, a sidewalk
is still a sidewalk: and I'm still the same):

                            (as for the painful dizzy spells
and migraines they warned me about at the Optical Institute on Corso Buenos Aires,
where I'd checked in, I suffered them and soldiered on): (the ophthalmologist
asserted that, over time, I had constructed my own arbitrary representation
of reality, now destined, with new glasses, to be shattered):

                                    (and I could
hope, for a moment, to remake for myself, at little cost, a life and a vision):

"when I swim inside you, freestyle"

when I swim inside you, freestyle (like a professional, almost: halfway
to not half bad, at any rate), I make like a submarine, hold my breath,
and (half-closing, closing my eyes) I extend my arms, I splay my legs,
I peel my banana (and put a hood on it):
                                          I play dead, I buckle, I sway:
that's it: (pentagonal and star-shaped, if you like, inscribable in my own circle):

from *Casket*

"I'm a Riace bronze"

I'm a Riace bronze (one of the two, the one you prize most): yet really I'm
just withered, stooped (and long in the tooth): (and shaved, skin-headed, skinned):
even if I seem, you see (and touch), more evolved, with an extra pinch of pecker:
I still exist in a rather primordial stage of restoration
(tumefied, encrusted, with the taint of corrosion and broken bones):
                                                    and I'm
cabled together, pulleyed up (my eyes all set, my teeth taken out, if I'm a B,
so be it):
            (at heart I'm an A, please, you don't say, puffed up with good stuff):

"in view of the fact"

in view of the fact that, in the past, I slid down the slide with you:
(played two little blackbirds): (and hot hands, leapfrog, and handy-dandy): (discarded
jokers and passed the trash): (played ninepins and cup-and-ball): (and Go Fish): (rode
rollercoasters and flicked roly-poly toys): (blew bubbles, spun tops): (played king of the hill,
kick-the-can, and scopa): (and scopone and cornhole): (and hopscotch):

in view of the fact

that it was for you I played foursquare: that I was cop and robber, racing
in your sacks, bartering at your carnivals, coming to you crying, I spy with my little eye:
(and I spun you round and round, mast of my greasy maypoles):

I declare

and confirm, in writing, that, by some stroke of luck, I'm the one, for eternity, for you,
eagle of my too many heads, blind man's bluff and charade, wedge for the beast with two backs:

"may it please the court"

may it please the court:

I confess, I went on record, somewhere, artfully, with this
story of mine: I play the clown in the square, on a stage: (I'm the tooth-puller,
I eat and breathe fire, I'm the contortionist tightrope walker, tamer of lions and fleas,
swindler with the secret potion, charmer of snakes, reader of Tarot packs and palms,
the gypsy, the straight man to Howdy Doody, the rake): (circled and pushed by a throng
of little Petrolini-like doctors, à la manière de Molière, with gigantic syringes
(and giant shoes with long laces) who spray right and left and all around me
a thick cloud of disinfectant deodorant):

I stick a hand in my mouth,
I reach deep down my throat, with my arm, onward and under, ever farther
inward, down, passe-passe of passe-partout, until I snatch, at the cul-de-sac,
with my finger (my index, mind you), the ring of my stretchy sphincter:
and tug hard, voilà: I turn my insides out, and I sort of look like a rabbit, skinned:
and I yell softly from my anus:

step right up and take a look: this is the naked man,
truth in the flesh, if you take him at his intimate innards (served au natural):

"in my life I've already seen"

in my life I've already seen blazers, beetles, an inferno upended by Doré,
cholera, colors, seas and marble stones: and a square in Oslo, the Grand Hôtel
des Palmes, bourses, busts:
                          I've already seen blackjack, anagrams, hecto-
grams, fruitcakes, racetracks, jackpots, monuments to Mazzini, chicks and children,
Ridolini:
         I've already seen the firing squads of the *Third of May* (reproductions only,
in black and white), the tortured in June, the massacred in September, the hanged in March,
in December: and my mother's sex and my father's: the void, veritas, unarmed
worms, and thermal spas:
                          I've already seen the neutrino, the neutron, the photon, the electron,
(in a graphic, schematic display): *The Pentamerone*, *The Esamerone*: the sun,
salt, cancer, and Patty Pravo: and Venus, and ashes, and mascarpone (or
maskerpone), and a mascaron, and the demi-cannon: and mascarpio (Lat.) to manus
carpere:
         but now that I've seen you, life, pluck out my eyes—enough:

58

from *Codicil*

"writing's what I do, not who I am"

writing's what I do, not who I am:
                          despite the bang-up job I do
(with fire and flames): (I do you and elicit your pity): (and I did dream the seven
dreams): (I do the happy routine, and I'm not happy): (for you I don the face you see):
(I do go on a bit, and step in shit, I get into all kinds of mischief): (my stride outdoes my leg span):
(I go a round in the ring, flexing my muscle): (and I go get lost and get bent):
(I mind my own beeswax, and my business): (I want it done right so I do it myself: for a lark):
(for something to do, and undo): (I do double duty, centuple, and I know what I'm doing):
(and finally I do myself in): not being writing, for the time being
I keep similitude in mind:
                          (and transmit it to this page):

"I emerge from your dream"

I emerge from your dream, from you (and me): I'm a soap bubble, a sponge: (the same sponge
you purchased at a perfume shop yesterday, here in Rivarolo, with me): (the bubbles
the washing machine makes in the kitchen when it spills over on high spin, rattling,
rattling us, epileptic):
     I'm whiter than white: (and full of special
offers and coupons and freebies and vouchers and prizes) (and toys and stickers):
(I'm portable, indispensable): (I can be raffled off): I seduce you three times, four (on sight):
(at first sight): (et à bout de souffle, i.e., breathless): I'm a stroke of lightning:
(a shot to the heart): (and a stroke of luck):
     me, your (half-baked) half moon:

"I remember my future like a nightmare"

I remember my future like a nightmare: and fail to prefigure my past: today,
not seeing myself and seeing myself, I see you, I think, and see you no more:

outdated

(dateless and toothless), I close my mouth around your tongue, squeeze your fingers
in my fingers: and cram them between my agonized knees, between my thick
thighs (over my sack of wormy nuts, over my pickled and icy
eel):

    I'm in your hands (in good hands): I tremble and take pleasure in them: (and
I spin and spill into them):

             and that's us, us, two souls disjoined and a single body:

Mauritshuis

Jan Sanders van Hemessen

that girl, tender but buff, who splashes and sprays me, spitting up clots
of her milk, squeezing her left nipple over my flimsy tenor viola
(yet doesn't deign to look at me), she's pursued me my whole life
with her billion braids (and all those leaves standing upright on her head
like a mohawk) just to touch me:
                                        and now she's done it: (and interrupted,
for the moment, my poor countryside solo): I lay down my bow: it's late:
(her intentions may be good): (but the terrifying, windswept shepherd
in the background is making, I think, a kind of sign
                                                    to beckon me):
                                                            I feel the shy
pitter-patter of drops from that bright brisk milkmaid: (then nothing any longer):

Pieter de Hooch

all right, you're right, I'm amusing: (let's leave my stockings out of it): and I bet
you failed to notice it's in my left hand I'm holding my pipe: (the other's on the table:
and if you insist, and if, as they say, it'll make you happy, I'll pick that one up
with my right hand after): (but for me, you always drink too much): (and, look,
no one looks at me): (on the other hand, everyone looks at you, with your door
open onto the street): (not even the tower sees me sitting here): (and now
I'll take my leave, as they say, I'm off): (yet here in the courtyard, a step away
from us, is our daughter, rigid, the frigid one: I don't get what she's got in her hand:
but it sure is clear she's sad to death):

because, anyhow, as

they say, ahem, I'm frittering my life away: I gambled and lost: (and now I smoke):

Frans van Mieris

here's a modest invitation to love, a clumsy bundle of mattresses, tablecloths, etc.,
hung up on the high ledge of the loft to take the air:
                                                      and here's another
invitation to love, farther back, the withdrawal of eternal figures (who pay us
no mind): (but, in any case, they're external to this luminous hut): (their whispering
must mean, I'm pretty sure, a tacit agreement, a pathetic plot, sweet pangs):
                                                                      and
here's a third invitation to love, a canine couple coupling (doggy-style, doggonit):
(in fact it was censored, veiled in violet, actually castrated):
                                                      but you, my fleshy
little vixen, who ignore sleeping beauty (and whose apron I'm pulling on on purpose),
you who reveal, loosening your bustier, a bit of your body (to whom I extend,
delicately with two fingers, my empty flute under your pitcher, and my mouth
to your empty mouth), slowly, prudently bending over: uh, you're nothing to me,
my pretty, my joy, but an invitation to love: you're love sans phrase (a colon, wham bam):

Rembrandt van Rijn

my name is Aris Kindt: I was a notorious criminal: (executed
by authorities of the age): (and, in the end, put to good use): I ask
of the connoisseur tourist setting his eyes on my rank limb (which looks,
woe is me, like a prosthetic glove, a phony plastic fiasco) neither
compassion nor pity for the skillfully calculated mess of my quiet

cadaver:

for me,

all that is engraved in the looks of those gentlemen posing
(perplexity and calm, discomfort and curiosity, horror and distraction
and worry) is consolation for eternity: (naturally, I thank Doctor Tulp
for his memorable lesson and his discreet, cordial gesture):

vive et vale:

Johannes Vermeer

according to the clock it's 7:10 a.m.: (I recognize the ports of Schiedam and Rotterdam):
(it must have rained in the night): and now I'm looking for certain little figures
in blue, and the pink sand: (and I ate undercooked potatoes): and now I'm looking
for a tiny yellow fragment of a wall with a canopy: I don't recognize the sky, it's too
wide: (I recognize I'm dying now):

                              et c'est ainsi que j'aurais dû t'écrire:

Joachim Wtewael

what's with all these people intervening, I'm screwing this upright lady (and they're
freaking me out): I understand her husband coming toward me, bowed, bare-assed,
to net me in the act:

                  but that guy leaping onto the bed, hanging sideways
from the canopy, wearing a red hat and carrying a stick (and that obscene boy
behind me), and the diver flying over me, pressed against the ceiling, his arms
spread out (and the blind, cockeyed old man cooped up in the corner with his friend
spying on me), and that guy (and girl) and that other one:

                                          it's too much:

                                                entirely desperate,
I hold out my hand to shield myself against the athletes hovering threateningly
above me: and I expect the worst, melancholic oaf that I am:

Pieter Claesz

think hard, daughter, on this dead watch (with its cerulean ribbon
and key), on this cup knocked over, on this widowed
                                        candle holder:
                                                    on my warped,
dusty notebooks, topped with that human bone heap, I set down
my semi-tapped, silenced quill: (it's a well-worn obligatory bag of tricks: yet it never fails
to animate): and it's true: everything here
                        is nothing:
                                        (and that nothing is everything):

from *Rebus*

"I discover the most different doubles"

I discover the most different doubles of the lost and missing everywhere:

from el Micalet to el Mercado

(take away two whiskers and, by chance, a nose, touch up the eyes, shorten
both knees), you run into them en masse every minute: (I nearly fainted):
(because it's crazy, if, if you think about it, a split self means nothing here: it results
in amiable indifference, cordial bureaucracy: people terrifyingly out of sync): (out of place
and out of tune): (and misshapen, even improved):

you're not here, you whom I miss, the only one:

"backing up, disheartened"

backing up, disheartened by a top-shelf bombshell, Rubens' brand, I stepped
on the fine foot of a woman exploring the Prado (excuse me, I said, embarrassed):
(and added an "enchanted," a "pleasure": to whom I said it, who knows, not me):
(I fly into trances and raptures for no reason: or rather, I get stuck, trip up,
revved, off-kilter, awed by framed flesh amid the muscle-mush of tourists):

                                                       (but
picture a strawman, falling where and how I fall, tossing and twisting, leaning
here and there, where and how I lean, in this ill-fitted trash bag stuffed with sawdust,
which emanates from me, which I emit):

                                   (phony, sewn shut, I'm a game gone too far):

"TOPIC"

TOPIC:

        you have become a grandfather: briefly explain your impressions, your
feelings, etc.:

        RESPONSE:

                when I first saw her, the afternoon of the 9th,
she was sound asleep on her stomach: (the usual arms half stretched out, her hands
making half fists): but when she woke up again, silently, after a while (she's taciturn
by nature, I think), she looked me over with great concern (almost scared,
poor thing), knitting her colorless hint of a brow:

                                (but then,
in an instant, I calmed her down with the practiced effects (and affections) of my voice,
tested, what now seems a century ago, on her father):

                            so that on future occasions
I might say that's how I made my presence felt, on the first take, with my serene,
unscathed eyes, to the offspring with my same eyes, pierced with delicate patience,
in a hereditary heterosexual micro-face, excessive eyes: (that hold fast):

"what do you do?"

what do you do? (they often ask me): I say nothing back (sometimes): or else
I say instead (sometimes): nothing:

                         other times I say: too many things to tell you
(but nothing that matters: and nothing that matters to me): (considering that,
shillyshallying, nothing matters to me): (I'm merely following, oftentimes,
this hushed hush-hush of a whisper whirring inside me, weakly, no longer even
turning into word, phrase, verse):

                    I seek an end, in the end:

from *Phanerographs*

La Philosophie dans le Théâtre

for Benno Besson

the intention was another, dear Benno: a *Paradoxe*, naturally ("sur
le metteur en scène," naturally), and now I have no time to write it down
for you: (yet the epigraph was the famous "si le petit sauvage" in *Le Neveu*, referring,
at the outset, to an Oedipus):
                I wanted to return to être sensible and feeling
(to affaire d'âme and affaire de jugement): I tried drafting, a while ago,
an author's paradox (writing in first person, living in third, like Brecht,
being un autre): by this route, we can arrive at our real question, I think
(quelle est la planète où l'on parle ainsi?): at a système de déclamation:
(and, in the end, a life system, maybe): and we are, I hope, the least sensible beings
in the world: (with no taste for virtue, no desire to be useful to society
or serve country or family: without motifs honnêtes of any kind):
(no esprit droit, no cœur chaud, no soul): I don't want to abandon myself
à la merci de mon diaphragm: (j'ai fait un aveu qui n'est pas trop ordinaire):
and the crux, see, is exagération:
                which is exactly why I exaggerate when I write you:
(on July 21, 1827, a Saturday, Goethe told Eckermann that terror
is the essence of every poem: and on July 26, 1826, a Wednesday, he also said
theatricality is symbolic):
            to reduce emotions to sensible sensations,
to wring conscience from our pores, popping it like a pimple
(and to incite fear, stimulating real mouths to ejaculate thoughts in a sludge
of words, and for words to be made flesh): (I think of a tragic orgasmic farce,
a tragic striptease of ideology: I think, see, of the obscene in the scene):
(grand boudoir of every philosophy):
                every theater is an anatomical theater:

Tombeau for Eusebio

as he was (and as, on rare occasions, he appeared to me in carnal clips,
like Super 8 stock footage) when he was alive (yet running backward, in the sober
shudder of a faint flash, as in a flashback, on the faded white veil of a bare black
backdrop showing the hereafter of a life in the afterlife), I saw he was at ease
(half-asleep, muttering a wheezy cabaletta over the whistles of diurnal bats
and stilnovisti: they were his signposts and senhals, mixed with bon mots,
motets, and ultrasound metaphors), under the diaphanous screen of his thin
epitaph (the scribe's futile sign off):

                                dead at five percent (or a little more):

from *Corollary*

"acrobat (n. masc.)"

acrobat (n. masc.): one who walks on the very tips (of his toes): (at least
that's its etymon): yet who also proceeds, effortlessly, on the very tips
of his fingers (and the tines of a fork): on his head: (and on a bed of nails,
fakiring and funambuling): (on tightropes strung across two houses,
through streets and squares: on a trapeze, in a circus, in a circle, up in the sky):
he twirls, pliantly, on two stilts slid into two cups, into two shoes,
into two gloves: (in smoke, in air): pneumatic and somatic, in thin air:
(in air-pumped tires, in barrels and bottles): and performs a fatal leap:
and a fatal (and moral) spin:

                       (I spin and leap like that, me, in your heart):

"carve them in block letters"

carve them in block letters, readers of my will (I'm talking to my students,
my hypocrite children, the pro-proletariats who resemble me to a T, now as countless
as grains of sand in my empty desert): these words of mine on my tomb,
do it with spit, swishing a finger in your mouths: (just as I'm swishing a finger
around the excessive abscesses of my icy gums):

                              my life, I lapped it up:

"split from you, I'm stripped of everything"

split from you, I'm stripped of everything:
                                    but the best (or worst) of me
still clings to you, sticky, like honey, glue, a thick oil: I come back to myself
when I come back to you: (and find my thumbs and lungs again):
in a little while I land in Madrid:
                                    (there's a sampling of my countrymen in the rear
of the plane, suits that tally up numbers, drinking, smoking, wound up,
laughing nervously):
                    I still live for you if I'm still alive:

"into this shoddy retiro"

into this shoddy retiro filled with fairground booths (a dancer in yellow and green and white was defying the mud, limply pirouetting), we fell, first three of us, then four: (the discovery of paper models—to cut up with desperate, entirely Iberian tenacity—and soft donuts—to dunk and gulp—occurred shortly after, with the wordless, lakeside quack-quacks, which are, on the other hand, universal):

> but it's late, it's dark out, they're closing down, and the taxi's on its way:

"all told (he wrote)"

all told (he wrote), existence, in general (we're in '26:
we're in the month of April), is a slight imperfection:
                                                            (slight,
of course, compared with the immensity of nonexistence, of nothingness
pure and simple): it's an irregularity, a monstrosity:
                                                            my voice, this way, my
writing, I know, horrifically disfigure (not for long now) the supreme
harmony of agraphia, of aphasia:
                                        (already I give up, dyslexic, rereading myself):

"so then, what are we (Italians) like?"

so then, what are we (Italians) like?
                              the question was tackled and assiduously
dissected one night over dinner at the Montefiore in Mishkenot with a few opulent
half-Bulgarians (and a hardy, half- or full-blooded Bulgaress):
                                                  (e.g.,
are we sensual? sexual? sensitive?): (are we sexually sound?): (soundly
sexed?): (in the end it all depends on the language you choose): (above all,
on the language you're subjected to): (and here, like exquisite passive fumes,
reams of implacable, passive photos (and implacable tongues) ravished you):
(and the passive tongue, you see, or sense, rather (you sense it sensorially if you sense it):
(if you sense the tongue): the tongue in itself is already an anxiolytic amphibology:
that is to say, sexually sound):
                      so went my last evening, my last supper:
as planned, it was a total sexy-booze and -schmooze:
                                          (a merry usque ad mortem):

"if you lived it over"

if you lived it over, what would you revise?

                                  nothing, frankly: (I'm beset with bitter remorse, sweetheart): (I'm a hair-raising encyclopedia of bullshit statements, semi-criminal super-gaffes: and my years amount to an incomparable collection of irremediable existential typos):

        yet frankly, I wouldn't touch a single comma, not a single period: (I'd be terrified of the domino effect): (change a gesture, a word: re-knot, for the hell of it, the knot of your necktie): (but what am I saying? one day you trim away nothing but an extra nose hair): (and you're playing with fate—fate: et tout se tient): (and suppose that, and set your mind to it: you were to disappear, then, from this new life I'd live, given a second go): well frankly:

                what I've had, I'll keep: (to keep you I'll keep me the same):

"dear proletarian comrade"

dear proletarian comrade,

                       I know a ways back along the way we nearly lost
the Fourth State, its class consciousness (though I sure hope not for good)
—but not the Third State, since the bourgeoisie is the bourgeoisie, its mind
is still sharp: and capitalism is capitalism: (is sovereign—is supreme):
(and there's little love left for communism nowadays, no doubt):

                                           but here
—here, for starters, we should vote against the liberties of lords and ladies:
against our servitude and chains:

                        we all have to straighten up a few old flags
that have fallen in the mud: (and reawaken, meanwhile, to our dream):

from *Things*

"what (I wonder)"

what (I wonder) do I seek in myself so that I run from myself, thus running, forever
at a gallop? it's me, I know: (my death): (a sweet death): (a sleep-with-the-fishes death):
(which isn't really coming for me, anyway): (and it's not as if it's right over my shoulder
now, probably not):
                  I run from my life (from you, meaning you're my life):
(if all this makes so little sense, what shall we do?): I run in me, I run in you:
in your world, in mine: (me, who once thought, to think, that I'd had everything in life,
having had you):
                when we arrive, we cry: safe!: (game over, for real):

"there's a piano bar"

there's a piano bar, it's true, in action here: (there's a blue pool kept under
polychromatic spotlights that make me semi-cross-eyed, semi-cinematically): (here,
this time, that means, semi-Felliniesquely, to the limit): (but the limit here is considerable):
(but here I'm missing a little polonaise-style boy): (half-choleric style):
he'd be convenient here, as long, however, as he were semi-beautiful (semi-
Viscontianly, in the avant mode, in the après deux guerres mode): (et avant et après
mille guerres, et aussi pendant, je sais, je sais

très bien):

so here I saw
an obscene show: (about Roman romancers, real romantics: really amoral, in fact):
life's damn hard: life's a really hard, excitable

cock and bull story:

(I love you, my love):

"my virtue was immodesty"

my virtue was immodesty:
                              (which I displayed right and left, continually;
the span of a life is long and wide, my colossal disgraces disgraceful): in the Golden,
the pub in the Park Hotel, San Juan jct., I'd be very liable and very likely
to fire off one of my public ejaculations, thinking of you, my faraway wife: (I strain
to restrain myself): (I cross my legs real tight, I slowly scratch my underwear,
I don't know where to put my hands anymore):
                              my one virtue was modesty:

"the categorical imperative says"

the categorical imperative says:
                              eat, drink, and, above all else, fuck:
(fuck as much as possible, for sure): (and as best you can, if you can):
(I spent a lifetime doing it to you): (and now I know I spent it well):
dear accomplice, wife: I'm a wolfish cat, and filthy, and full of mirth:

"my message to you is this"

my message to you is this:

                  greater-than colon minus open parenthesis (>:-():

you answer me thus:

              colon minus d (i.e., uppercase d) (:-D):

                                I copy you

and add:

      a colon and asterisk: and closed parenthesis (:*)): and then colon
and apostrophe minus open parenthesis (:'-():

                        but you revise yours, finally, a tad,

with colon minus open parenthesis (:-():

                    after a colon, at this point, I'm a forward

slash, and I slip, in the middle, a minus sign (:-/):

                         and now, BYE: I won't net you

or chat with you again (I repeat: BYE and BYE): MUTE, I SCREAM THE SILENCE:

from *Any Other Business*

Little Threnos

the rooms you live in now (now, I mean, that you live in them, all and utterly
alone at this point) are full of music: (of your music, I mean): (of you,
who have been music, for me, for everyone, for years and years, here):

(I imagine a kind
of musique d'ameublement, as they used to say, de tapisserie): (and your old telegram,
which read, I think, "THANKS," and nothing else, will have arrived for you
this time): (and outside, flowers are flowering, Talia told me, yesterday):

(and,
sure, you'll have immediately verified that there's no god, no goddess, anywhere):
(not even a mini Camena of music, I mean nothing): (and, I don't know, I picture you
a little more at ease that way):

(but you knew, it's written in stone, that mortals
aren't allowed (shouldn't be allowed, I mean, anyways) to weep for immortals, not ever):
(yet if that's the reason, then leave it to us, here, now, fortunately, perforce):

Notes

Reisebilder

"At 6:15 p.m. Vasko phones": Vasko Popa (1922–1991): Serbian poet. Knaak-Poetry: a festival of popular poetry held in Rotterdam. "Knaak" is Dutch slang for "cheap" and derives from the name for the silver 2½ Gulden coin.

"where are the forty poets": Tadeusz Różewicz (1921–2014): Polish poet, playwright, screenwriter, and novelist. Yehuda Amichai (1924–2000): Israeli poet. Dolle Mina (or "Mad Mina"): the name of a group of feminist activists in the Netherlands in the 1970s.

"I'm more Slavic than Tadeusz": *The Criminal Life of Archibaldo de la Cruz*: 1955 Mexican film.

"the two corpses displayed in the basement": Michele: the poet's third son.

"I'd never heard so many hallelujahs": Spandauer Damm: a street in Berlin. "Und da objekt so rein als nur zu tun wäre in mich auf zunehmen," from Goethe's autobiographical writings, roughly means: "to absorb the object into myself as purely as possible."

"August 1st (a Sunday)": Gerald Bisinger: an Austrian poet and editor who translated works by several of his Italian contemporaries, including Sanguineti.

"the ugly purple corpse I lug behind me": The poet's childhood home in Turin was located on Corso Matteotti.

Postkarten

"put it back on its feet, the culture": Teatro Eliseo: a landmark theater in Rome.

"let's talk, please, about life's pleasures": Frans van Rossum: producer for the Dutch Radio Station KRO. Luciano Berio: experimental Italian composer. He collaborated frequently with Sanguineti, who provided the texts—largely collages of literary quotations—for compositions, including *A-Ronne* and *Coro*.

"this pillow is a butterfly": *Orlando*: opera by Friedrich Handel. *I Masnadieri*: opera by Giuseppe Verdi.

"the final account on the return flight": Doelen: concert hall in Rotterdam that was home to the Poetry International Festival from 1970–1996. Octavio Paz (1914–1998): Mexican poet. Marie Jose Tramini: artist and Paz's widow.

"to prepare a poem": Pellegrino Artusi (1820–1911): Italian author of *The Science of Cooking and the Art of Fine Dining*. Luigi Carnacina (1888–1981): Italian hotel manager and co-author of *Great Italian Cooking*.

"my father's voice is recorded": Federico: the poet's firstborn.

Scratchpad

"I live like a mouse": "Inst": an obsolete abbreviation used in commercial language to refer to the date of the current month. From Latin, "instante mense."

"I began your Chinese notebook": *Les Aventures de *** ou Les Effets surprenants de la sympathie:* 18th-century dramatist Marivaux's picaresque debut novel.

"I'll return to my last poem": The original version begins "ritorno sopra la 34" (I'll return to #34), the number 34 referring to "a slogan slipped" in the original.

"I'm a Riace bronze": The Riace bronzes (or Riace Warriors): two life-size Greek bronze statues discovered off the coast of Riace Marina, Italy, in 1972. The statues are commonly referred to as "Statue A" and "Statue B."

"may it please the court": Ettore Petrolini: Italian stage and screen actor in the early 20th century, famous for having created iconic character sketches.

"in my life I've already seen": Ridolini: the Italian name for Larry Semon, an American comic actor of the silent film era.

Mauritshuis

Mauritshuis is a group of seven poems written in 1986 after Sanguineti visited the eponymous Dutch museum. Each poem responds to—and reimagines—a particular painting in the museum's collection. Below is a list of the paintings in order of appearance:

Jan Sanders van Hemessen, *Allegorical Scene,* possibly the *Personification of Poetry with a Poet,* c. 1550.

Pieter de Hooch, *A Man Smoking and a Woman Drinking in a Courtyard,* c. 1658–60.

Frans van Mieris, *Brothel,* c. 1658–59.

Rembrandt van Rijn, *The Anatomy Lesson of Dr. Nicolaes Tulp,* c. 1632.

Johannes Vermeer, *View of Delft,* c. 1660–61.

Joachim Wtewael, *Mars and Venus Surprised by Vulcan,* c. 1601.

Pieter Claesz, *Vanitas Still Life,* c. 1630.

Phanerographs

"La Philosophie dans le Théâtre": *Rameau's Nephew* (*Le Neveu de Rameau*): satirical philosophical dialogue written by Denis Diderot in the 18th century.

"Tombeau for Eusebio": Eusebio: Genoese poet Eugenio Montale's nickname. In his *Diario del '71 e del '72,* Montale wrote that he "lived at five percent." Senhals: pseudonyms used by Provencal poets to conceal the true identity of a lady, a practice Montale employed in his own work.

Things

"the categorical imperative says": Sanguineti's nickname, "wolfish cat" (in Italian *gatto lupesco*), comes from an anonymous Florentine poem, *Detto del gatto lupesco* ("The Sayings of the Wolfish Cat"), in which the titular hero sets out on a quest to seek the truth from everyone he encounters. *Il Gatto Lupesco* is also the title of Sanguineti's selected poems (1981–2001).

Any Other Business

"Little Threnos": The poem is dedicated to the memory of Luciano Berio, who was married to Talia Pecker Berio from 1977 until his death in 2003.

Acknowledgments

I'd like to thank the editors of Oberlin College Press: Kazim Ali, David Walker, and David Young. Special thanks to Martha Collins for her close reading of the manuscript.

I'd also like to thank the editors of the following journals in which some of these translations previously appeared: *Agni, Circumference: Poetry in Translation, Drunken Boat, FIELD, Poetry Northwest, Plume,* and *Two Lines Press.*

For encouragement, heartfelt thanks to Michael Collier, Theo Collier, Miriam Grottanelli, Michael F. Moore, and the late Mark Strand.

Thanks to John Picchione for clarifying a few allusions and helping provide a critical understanding of Sanguineti's work and the new avant-garde in Italy.

Finally I'd like to thank my wife, Tania Biancalani: "se d'amore si vive, siamo vivi…"

This book is made possible by grants from the National Endowment for the Arts and PEN/America, as well as the Jeannette Haien Ballard Writer's Prize, the Reginald S. Tickner Fellowship, and the Amy Lowell Poetry Travelling Scholarship.

The FIELD Translation Series

1999   Max Jacob, *Selected Poems* (translated by William Kulik)

2001   Vénus Khoury-Ghata, *Here There Was Once a Country* (translated by Marilyn Hacker)

2004   Eugenio Montale, *Selected Poems* (translated by Jonathan Galassi, Charles Wright, and David Young)

2005   Inge Pedersen, *The Thirteenth Month* (translated by Marilyn Nelson)

2006   Herman de Coninck, *The Plural of Happiness: Selected Poems* (translated by Laure-Anne Bosselaar and Kurt Brown)

2009   Emmanuel Moses, *He and I* (translated by Marilyn Hacker)

2011   Georg Trakl, *Poems* (translated by Stephen Tapscott)

2013   Pierre Peuchmaurd, *The Nothing Bird: Selected Poems* (translated by E. C. Belli)

2016   Emmanuel Moses, *Preludes and Fugues* (translated by Marilyn Hacker)

2018   Edoardo Sanguineti, *My Life, I Lapped It Up: Selected Poems* (translated by Will Schutt)